(aviary)

(aviary)
Genevieve Kaplan

velizbooks.com

Veliz Books' titles are available to the trade through our website and our primary distributor, Small Press Distribution (800) 869.7553. For personal orders, catalogs, course adoptions, or other information, write to info@velizbooks.com

For further information write Veliz Books:
P.O. Box 961273, El Paso, TX 79996
velizbooks.com

ISBN 978-1-949776-06-5

Cover design by Silvana Ayala

CONTENTS

***

The birds had taken over

and that was enough pleasant talk
a chirp, there
a peck and a scattering of seed
and they get smarter by the hour, defined
by the sun and the shadow
the leaves that appear on the dead-looking tree
the breeze that flicks the branches
the setting sun
the at-last-unforeseen black wing
of the bird searching under the elevated
joint of the railing
the angle of the earth
that is summer, is spring. is one moment left, one
dream-world in slanted shade
one swipe of light in the eyes, one place
for birds to assemble, to trim
the branches. an upset of the flock
and a new one settles, talks
back, is a clear day, or a sign
that evens out, an assertion from the next mile over
the birds are prone to jostling
and feed extravagantly

A swift (quick) justice

the birds in the yard swooped up
by the other birds
in the yard. the predatory (preliminary)
birds. a cache of feathers rusting
alongside the bicycle
a thump in the outer foyer
what they did was wrong, no doubt
and where, and how. and the kind
of flapping, which shouts—I won't
be fooled again. this was one
last time that I tried. one brush
over the fence—I could
hear you sweeping. the servile
mode of it. (to say I'm home
alone)—the drifting touch of it, impulsive
lift of it. each one we remember. (each
light wing, approached and approaching)
the thought I was about to have
(that one). you. here. the branches
rushing wildly. and over
the fence. and beyond the next
fence. and even
the concrete fence (the certain word
for it), beyond that, where some
of us live, beforehand
unafraid and that is almost enough

Apart from its pleas

enough the night, the low murmurs
that rise out and up. there aren't many words
fresh leaves, there's dirt beside the hedge, dug
from underneath. the horn
and the lights at night, the moon
and the heat of it. and accurate
disturbing calm. I shared with you then?
or *I shared with the tree, the hearth held*
for me. at night a pause and a cry
a skinny back. a loaded leaf. it's that place
that wanders and calls out. it's that scrawny
bird which wanders, scrapes, and calls out
and the lot of it cools
                                who will hold
out, having recently arrived, having sat
on the stoop with the bird, left the bird alone
on the stoop, and turned out the light

If they want to feed, it is theirs

if the moths get into it, then everyone eats
the morning coming, its clouds
(the one bird bigger than the morning)
but the smoke settles in and we're breathing
the birds and I, and the house
in the room, in the day
on the raised surface that is mine

daring, persistent, not about to panic—
might we, for their heckling
and grousing, their caterwauling slid
between the door and the doorjamb
and the sill
they babble on, lay claim
to the branches
pick
at the mess
of seed on the ground

To keep them in the dirt is by design

a scattering the leaves (like footsteps), the way I
had envisioned, I wouldn't be able to bite, underserved
(and gnawing), the chicken flapping on the roof, calling down
to me, not about to be alone at this (or actually paralyzed
by its motion). the sky turns white as if (as if a blind)
we could crouch and hide. peek out from
(the breeze) the mess of branches. it's a sleek
furtive wing that flies near. it wants to taunt, to get caught

you're from a far-off place, according to your eyes
and you'll never be able to name all the birds here
crumb of sunlight through the fence-slat and push of dust
against the patio. which is where we're at? sullen desert?
as big a yard as we could want? something near us
taking place? not about to let go? for this day
to be shorter than the rest. this this day to be easier
and far enough from what suffers us

Each day (a new needle on the gravel)

the largest bird is the one to return, brown
over white rocks, beak up
over the branches (I find
some loose feathers there). too bad
the evening can't support it (*a happiness*
gesture, sounds that spill out all together)
often we can't smell the sea here, often enough
the tops of the mountains appear. each morning
I peek out to see who is there. which legs
under the edge of the fence, whose throat
sounds, whose sad life. I don't think
the birds notice. I don't expect they remember
one day to the next, one bird gone after
they know where to go, but what, what, often too tight
in the head, not enough room between the eyes. the shadows
the tree, the low chirp, it would do
to make things happen, the air and the thick
of it, we're equally tired, too unamused
to look out for beauty, to see something in destruction
(a mining operation, a man-made pit—out, out)
unpeaceful falling, asleep even, at the time when it mattered

Wall-climber, ducker-underer

today does not reveal any difference, any motive
in the afternoon, the sparking
of a plan, we call to complain, we push
our faces through, we sit in the crest
of sunlight, we hold on to the fix in the air, we listen
for it

I'm all too close to stopping to listen

the hush beyond the fence
it's full of webs
it's a voice, after all
there's a body there. there's
the thing I want, the there, there. you
hear it too, you've got a broom. you claim
you'll take care of it, cricket
in your hand, bird on your shoulder, a regular
man, a tall solid man. and I know
it's yours, too

Or everything's washed away

we look, but there's nothing past the slats
even the growl is gone, the net. the next time
a drop doesn't hesitate
but falls (against it all). the tree drapes
over the edge. it reaches the crest
of the roof I think
it holds the birds. (for the danger is under
the overhang, in the window, near the glass
in the scatter of debris and how one leaf straddles
the fence line. how it's on both sides. and is
the thick of it.) there's no use
for the fruit, none for the leaves (other, none
other) as the birds decline
as they come and go in the powerless
evening, adjusting and reforming
from all the way above

Thin-hipped they arrive

a skittering across the roof, the wind
and the needles fall, the piles
against the corners, the barrier attracts (confines them
after all). as part of the slip (from it), as the gesturing
downward, crumbling, the movement against
the tree shakes, the leaf-dwindle, the house. (admired
but chased is tricky, and the cat dashes for the door)
                                          the moon
(the fragment there) stands it well enough, but the birds
think it is night (they hide), they refuse
to make their noises. they decide against it, and that they must
return. that they must attract. (and that they must eat. flight
blind, they come for the sound, talon-tipped.)

those details and their lost subjects. their movements
layered through the glass, the glass
(that is their houses). built in many locations, for many
sets of eyes. and if one walks in, one risks it. one is tall
enough, but one can't reach. one stands
on the brick. one stretches up. one shifts its arch
over the leaves (one sees a pattern there), one tries
                                          the branches shock
in the moonlight, and the tree leafs down, and it's evening
and it's quiet and one tried. and one sat
down. and one watched

Part of this season

the birds ignore such goings-on, their interest
is in leaves, the branches, the color
of the sky each night, I think
there's a sound (there is
and there's not. and there is) and there isn't
some play. the concrete sky, the cement of the ground
it's all one structure. and it holds
together. we hear the metallic tap of their beaks
the clink a foot makes along the edge, around
the edge of the ring. it's too still, in the vein
of the sun, it highlights
only a dry leaf, and another dry leaf and
another. you read it in the way the tree
leans toward us, how the smaller tree fruits
but doesn't ripen, how the metal glints
stirring spokes and dust and I listen
for what's coming. I hope to improve
the brick. I hope not to lose sight of the slats
I think I'll be able to hold it again if I look closely

The birds browner, the sky bluer, the branches

we'd guess it from the way the leaves shifted—something off
about the weather. the birds browner, sky bluer, branches crossing all
at odd angles. the leaves pushed to the side, the affected piles
(and the rush of wind, a deep breath, in the distance) don't hold it
over them. look at the ground
                              and there, which is dirt, are the shot
seeds. the arm almost touches the rail of the roof. someone sent it—it
arrived so we watched—so we took it. down, past the sweep
of the broom. organized in such a manner—one close angle, then one
far, and one disputed. a leaf hanging bitterly if not pushed
to the ground. its cause to lean? never, never obvious

The pattern of their beating wings

the instinct is to hurry as the light fades
which is the pattern of their beating
the pattern (the arc) left behind by its beating
its proud head. it watches and it's shunned (it leaps
but can't fly) (footsteps and they all flew). one poses
on each branch, one keeps
its feet

I'm there the moment it begins

we could still and watch it
o and there and quiet
we could shift and listen
to the picking, the feet and the beak
and the will. five rise
and fly off over. the yard, the branch
the callous living they do. the scenic
expectation, the calming of the sky
and the reach of the twigs
above their heads. they pick
they pick they shuffle they get
chirped off
or let loose from the yard

it is night falling
it is from outside, it is the yowl
of the (keening) animal beyond
the fence, looking in, gazing through

it is the undeveloped (dead)
the lost there, the desire
against the fence, beneath
the tree. we were all struggling
we were looking for something
together. an evening, a holding
a tree top, a vantage point
(to better understand the workings
of the system). to see the dark
to hear within it, to watch what passes
(and not be too terribly disappointed
to have missed it, to have missed
our chance), to keep
from being angry against it

In the morning, a different feeling

(softness?) with one drop on the tip
of each branch and small
growing things beneath. shush
of water in the (somewhat distant) streets
breath of it up and over the fence
but still a still leaf. one
(almost) hazardous chirp. time
that goes by in the (breast)
of the bird

                    to see
what he'll find (or if he'll return)
in the clasp of weather (a storm
a morning), the diminished sodden flight
in the gray, of the bells in the distance
of the tiny bird itself on the horizontal
branch (of the fenceline that is
the horizon) or humor here
in the damp field, the damp tree

the one bird of the morning, the soft sound
(surrounded by gray, steeped
in the branches) out the window, beyond the door
the quiet bird, the rain bird, the sun bird
peeks out not aloft, attracts, pulls tight
and then releases. drift by the kitchen, patter
at the pane. the sound glides along
with the noise of the train. nowhere
is silence, abstract, something small
footsteps. roof prattle. a morning call

The windows, the fence

if I hadn't been able to begin it, if the springtime
hadn't come, the shoots hadn't put
us to it—secret digging in the garden, down
upon wings, creating the new
undergrowth. the notion, listen: a siren
astride the bare branch. a reflection
off the web along the glass, the one smudge that glistens. home
the last place, the fenced place, we
let ourselves suffer its motion, limited
by the holding line, the sun
creeping, the shade. the lure of the soft
petal, a bird that stays, enough of the bud, the branch
to root. smooth versus dirt, landing versus taking
flight. the windows aren't enough. the fence surrounds the yard
and is too tall. (the drainpipe stopped, even.) rivals, these branches
allowed their reach, animals their roam. what
of the distance, only rooftops, treetops, fortressed
out, undebatable, taunting limbs (and limping.)

***

(ladies in an aviary)

a flat lovely sugar trail
a flock lump sugar tremor
a flutter man sugar up
a folded, man, sweep us
a for massive sweet us
a forgotten modest tassels values
a fringe. more than veneration
a frosted naïve that very
agitate gas nasty that visitor
among get of that waiting
an glistening of the what
and globes of the while
and great of the who
and groups of the whole
and hands, of the wings
and here of the wires
"angels," higher. of the wistfully
are his of the with
are holding of the with
as hour-glass on the woman's
as if on the would
as impatience on the you
as in on the
as in out. their
as in out their
aspiration, in poufs, their
at in pouting their
aviary in. recompose their
azaleas. in relief. their
be?" inquire replies, their
be inquisitive retiring. them
breasts into ribbon, these
brings is rise there
burns is ruffles they
bustles is running they
cage. is satin they

cannot is satisfied; they
close it sedately they
clouds, it settle they
cries it shadows this
curves it shift this
diamond lacy so throws
dispelling ladies so 'tis
down lashes solitaires to
eat ladies, soul to
existence. lift star to
feathers light starry to
fictitious like strong to
figures look sugar to
fingers love, sugar to

They are so lovely and they cannot get out

similarly, the light fades, thickens, and the moon
twice as big. if there are bars, if the key is lost
the sky is not affected. (this, a world where women
watch women, there are cages, creatures). as
a last night, final evening, or dusk in the mist
(of all fortune, rings shining there, dressed
improperly after all, in un-serious shoes) before
the park closes, we're no longer welcome, I pretend
to pass along, to gather slowly, to walk the parking lot
toward my own, watching

similarly the bed creaks. the tree blossoms, the radishes
twice their size. a bare skill to begin: women
and their children, a rake and a hoe. loose rattlings
of the daylight, an afternoon in spades. the bird turns
on its own, the ground beneath is moving. subtle ways
the shade extends, the minimum of (a human being)
the smallest gesture of (nature) inverted in springtime
the wet rocks, the hose that goes on, the house butted up
to a buzzing garden. what shade of blue? which brown? how
to get outside enough to see myself looking in?

That flat look at the naïve

and the gathering around was (the wires), the spit
on the ground, the fence so tall (the way it is) and now
encloses. as they look but don't want to show
as their friends arrive. as a group of them
gathers squatting, rolling. so unbeautiful. not
so left behind, the lot, the fortunate sunset (how) (at that
hour). and would it matter, the dirt for growing, the asphalt
for heating up. not so threatening, young man, the almost-shade
of the wisp-fence. in the not-quite of evening. spinning
(but controlled. departing with a close eye) a stained
fabric. a single-file walk (I follow behind. I look down)
(evenly) to the car. flat plane of a hand, outrageous
calm, smooth growth of the concrete. the fence stakes taller
even than the tallest broadest one. wires so thin they could be cut
(they could be cut) with what we brought

(in an aviary)

ladies in   of feathers
an aviary "angels," as

      their visitor inquisitive
they are so, replies, ladies

lovely and holding the running to
they cannot sugar higher. eat out of his

get out. and a flock hands
their of satin agitate these

breasts are curves settle tassels of the
pouting as on poufs, as soul in their

they trail if on clouds, impatience
their lacy waiting, to be

bustles with wings satisfied
among the sedately and it is very

azaleas. folded, for a wistfully
dispelling diamond star that they

the shadows to rise in a recompose
of their massive their ruffles

lashes in a fringe. on retiring
starry

      veneration, "here is
they lift that love," cries

flat look at the great
the naïve to strong man

the man who "'tis a
bring sugar woman's

to the cage whole
        existence."

it is so sweet and this
this sugar, lump of

fictitious more
values. glistening

        than the gas
"What in groups of

would you frosted
like us to globes as it

be?" they burns with a
inquire in a light as

flutter of forgotten to
modest us as the

aspiration, hour-glass
while the figures it

solitaires on throws into
their fingers relief

shift up and   they are so
down the there is a lovely and

wires that tremor of they cannot
close them ribbon, a get out

in. nasty sweep their
breasts are curves settle tassels of the

pouting as on poufs, as soul in their
they trail if on clouds, impatience

their lacy waiting, to be

It is so sweet this sugar, the sugar

and it meant something and it meant something to me
soothing in the springtime though the seeds eaten

and it meant something and it meant something, something
in the springtime, through the seeds, prowling out the night time
windows open, sash ajar, novices out (outshone) the bars, the slats
not so far away as we would like. soft (no). a hiss
to the monument of dusk coming quickly. how ought
I introduce it? how might it to me? soft time of the world, soft
hour of the hard night

(vary)

aviary

burns, bustles

clouds, cries, curves

diamond

eat, existence

feathers, fictitious, figures
fingers, flat, flock
flutter

forgotten, fringe, frosted

glistening, globes, great
groups

if

inquire

lacy, ladies, lashes
ladies, lift

love, lovely, lump

man, man, massive

naïve

poufs, pouting

recompose, relief, replies
retiring, ribbon, rise
ruffles, running

satin, satisfied, sedately
settle, shadows

sugar, sugar, sugar
sugar

A flutter of modest aspiration

as I thought I could pick it up, thought I could pick some up, watched
the birds hop through the wide wire of the fence, happily, like it was nothing
watch the weeds grow in their rows, watch
the stalks thicken, the calls
over the next fence, childish coos, the parking lot
separating us (up), the squirrel there, the children
in a line, the bird posing with its feet
on the wire, the sun, happily. as if to own a word, as if to live off the land

as if to shake it down, reach in through the bent wires and ease
up a leaf, (adjust) a stem (of a vegetable), to be seen from the porch
across the way, to hear the voices carry through (angry), through. as if
I could pick them up, as if I had brought
my gloves, if the key opened the other door, if the pile of dead leaves
was more than for (mulch). and sending messages
into the upper air. and waiting
for them to drift back down. because that's the morning
and the afternoon of it. the memorization
of that (cut sea), the memorial of that day, the grass
dug up, the site closed off but unprotected, that similar duty of my hands
my feet. the same sea I wandered through, the same lot

and I wouldn't know what to teach them, and I wouldn't
be able to want to be seen, and I'd reach
for the bird to tell it, wait, I dreamt (it for) you

(ladies)

they are so lovely and
their breasts are pouting among
the azaleas. dispelling the shadows
they lift that flat look

who brings sugar—it is
so sweet

they inquire while their fingers
shift up and down

and this lump of sugar
burns with a light
it throws into relief

Shift up and down the wires (that close them in)

mountain green, meadow green, antique green

which is the hedge which is not the fence which is where
we walk which is where we must stay out. that which
is the wind, that which fades. the tree an arch of the sky (to)
the sky. as leaves fall. as branches crack (the wind). and down
and a small tail showing through the tall grass. (because
there's a joke, there's a man) in the jungle green, the jungle
brown. the muddle yellow. the leaves are loud. and someone
always sneaking up from behind. the depression (in)
the ground, seated in this new place

which green was what I heard out in the yard. the fracture
of a branch or step. small movement of the night, glancing
toward the laundromat, the cartridge, electric types
of noises through the foliage, and someone coming closer, some
movement not so distant. as the order is the thing, the archiving
of the thing, the crickets and their pledges in the lost circle
of black-green. jungle there, at the shape of it, for the shape
near the trunk and the dirt of it. seemingly lost or broken fast
(to be unrecognizable), the main thing is to take the time
not near enough a breeze. or a tree motion, the night
which shadows on and (lingers) on

Holding the sugar higher

the white reaching-up in the breeze, tiny
hummingbird near the purples, for the bees
to take, to grasp the sun (to shake it off), skittish
by the passing of an orange machine, the greens
hazing for what sounds here, for not a love
not, as someone is always stepping. the bird
comes back, the bee, the voices come along. am I
alone here? no. (and the longer, the less so)

the handkerchief flitting there, the surrender
so the animal sounds, the machine, the human
silence comes, they veer right or left (the wrong
way), they find the dead end, the no-trespassing
yard. and the wires so tall, crossed only by (birds)
and they've stopped because they're so turned
because of the spider webbing the slats
of the bench (and the machine doesn't care
there, the sugar-field (beneath the squirrel-tree), all
upturned saucers, all (church-going) bonnets, all
the very hat upon my head, taller than my very
shoulders. so the wrestling in the branches
shifts their upright stance, (earthly) stoicism, their moon-
gesture in the sunshine. the footfalls, the leaves
on the ground, the machine choking up the path. the steps
downward, cut into the hill and angled purposefully. and I
am surrounded)

(in aviary)

they they cannot get out
their they trail their lacy
bustles the shadows of their
lashes lift that flat look
at who brings sugar to
the sweet this sugar, the
sugar would you like us
to a flutter of modest
aspiration, their fingers shift up
and close them in. "angels"
their sugar higher. and a
flock on poufs, as if
on sedately folded, for a
diamond a massive fringe. "here
is strong man," 'tis a
woman's lump of sugar is
more in groups of frosted
globes a light as forgotten
to figures it throws into
relief. of ribbon, a nasty
sweep ladies, running to eat
out these tassels of the
soul be satisfied; and it
is recompose their ruffles on
retiring

Waiting, with wings

as there is clearly something in the undergrowth
moving in the tree, the chortle
the caw. thrush of a bump up from behind (as the woodland
settles). the dirt grinds, the mud
does not reflect some voices, some of these branches
breaking, if I wait. what
is less empty streambed (barrel cactus), squirrel in the tree
and if they win? (if the spot
is not mine, after all on the path up the hill. someone
wins. someone's voice
rattles deep in the throat) someone climbs. the light
of the page burns, so blurs, so
is heavy on the eyes—vapor in the air never aids
for adjustment, hurrying along
opening up to the heat (of the day) (of the afternoon)

we feel it in every direction, even shy
lift of the hair, shy pushing it out of the eyes
(as there's something about being alone. some shout
about it, from afar, or not so far away). tiny orange-striped
white flower on the low bush, something to the effect
of which, which forms the effect of, a single blossom
at the top of the stalk: mustard, sagebrush, squat
palm (in the foothill woodlands, the oak forest)

The great strong man

under the tallest tree, inside the largest forest. with a halo of nets
in the clearing, from the path (from the stand), our boundaries
surround us. despite what we read, the railings, the beautiful
shade, the cracks wide enough to squeeze through. (the ever-widening
holes. we could gaze there forever)
                                        will benefit from some time away
perhaps, drinking in the green and brown so nothing would be stronger
then, broader than, the selection (of trees) we see here, no pity. no passing
without looking up. no silence from the stream. and the movement
in the trees, the rustle in the ground, picking up the (nails. the strewn things)
and so I would begin to disappear
                                        the angles lit-up and the fence poles (arms)
(abutting our very site. what we've determined is common ground) in the place
we've sent ourselves (to grow a little older in), to peer from, the waiting
room (abounding with gnats. the flit of the moth and the mosquito)
forgot to be shameful. forgot to hide since we see through to sky
all here together, tree, they could see us

(ladies a a a)

cannot as the lashes flat man (who brings sugar to the cage.)
the (sugar of fictitious values.)
be?" modest fingers (that close them in.)
sugar curves clouds, a massive (fringe.)
strong And glistening frosted light hour-glass (figures it throws into relief.)
a ladies, hands, in it their (ruffles on retiring.)

and Their they among shadows starry flat to sugar (to the cage.)
this fictitious (values.)
us in aspiration, their down them (in.)
holding a settle on sedately star massive (fringe.)
the a this more in as light as throws (into relief.)
of of running his of impatience it they (recompose their ruffles on retiring.)

so they out. are they lacy the the their starry lift look naïve man sugar (to the cage.)
so sugar, of (fictitious values.)
you to inquire flutter aspiration, solitaires fingers and wires them (in.)
visitor the And of settle as clouds wings for star in (fringe.)
love," great "'tis whole this sugar glistening gas of as with as us hour-glass throws (into relief.)
a ribbon sweep as running out hands, tassels soul impatience satisfied; is that their (retiring.)

out. lacy their look (sugar to the cage.)
of (fictitious values.)
inquire solitaires wires (that close them in.)
And as for (a diamond star to rise in a massive fringe.)
"'tis sugar of as (throws into relief.)
sweep out soul is (retiring.)

More glistening than the gas

the fog banks here and makes the trees unsteady. knots in each branch
or the leaves intertwine, with tendrils aiming up the rough bark
toward the opening (oblong, smoothed in, for bees) to move things along
(past the distant voices, through the slats of the bench here) the missing
thread, pole lopped off and left its gaping rung to be overtaken
(swallowed) by the garden. not down the ravine but in a (windswept)
clearing, coast oak, gray squirrel, competent weeds (a buzzing
up in the trees and from the bush behind, a twirling ratchet to cut
us off, dissuade us from entering the (beyond) (around
the corner)) circling with barbs, signs, and there's something picking
invisibly through the bark on the ground behind the looseness of the green
(pointing upwards) (the dropped lily). as if the gray is everywhere
reflected from the ground (the dirt) the leaves and the motions
gone behind. the step alongside (out from the path), the movement below
where the road goes outside this curve. see—a silver of bark littering
(with its sweet-smelling ashes) the tossed rocks (pointing) through
the gestures of spent leaves in the wind, the tree tipped but still
growing against the ground (the wall it forms)

(a vary)

They   they cannot   they trail
among the azaleas.   their lashes   they lift
      to the cage

    so sweet   sugar

                  they   flutter
                      the wires

"Here is love,"   And   more

as it burns   as the hour-glass   throws
into relief

There is a tremor   of feathers

    in their impatience   they recompose

           they recompose

A tremor of ribbon

the creek brushing past or the rocks
that surround it, the path wavering
up the low hill, dotted (strewn, bent)
with dry leaves in the slight wind
that comes to turn the trees, show
them off, lean them down. the bench
from which to watch, the spinning leaf
the wandering hair, the shudder from above
(against the click of the mechanical, the chains
strung up together, married, like people do)
the sign which informs, the letters to reveal
us—each lift in the rock a purposeful (irony)
a faceless opening. the net under the grass
(to catch us if we shift about) (empty
streambed, useless container, rainwater collector)
as the voice moves along down the path, stop
and sway, pause and look, point on a favorite
so unapologetic. rhododendron! (the type
of shout that travels) the poem that stabs
despite inaction, that pauses to pose
in silhouette and bounds forward, body
like a bending river, body is a short-haired
animal and uncomfortable in being so observed

It is very wistfully that they recompose

though not the bees and the grasshoppers (small ones
here), though not in the shade. they've tried all the routes, (lusted)
after hummingbirds, were bored by the rocks (again
and again). for who could not suppose to come (the ratio
of it all, the water filtering in (through the dirt
on the leaves)) and the (lone) bee (tumbling) over
pine needles arranged across the dust—just so
the slow progress and the false entrapment, the same day
of last week, the same day of tomorrow, the false
wildness, and then, when I turn my head away (after
the certain things we need, the water, the angles
of a shadow). and so I (we, they) was not alone, without
children, without having to stop and duck and point
here is the tiny school, the miniature library, the leaves
that shine in the sun and fold up in the shade. I couldn't
stand to look at them blowing with the wind, wavering
there, one leg propped against the other (four freckles
on the knee), so enclosed in this single space—I think
someone else would want to see (come in?) what is
most important beneath the sky, on the gravel, where
there is so little happening. which could take hours (defined
by monkey-flower, hanging by a birds-nest thread) and not
enough to be dreamt about, or spoken to (or spoken of) in that slow voice

***

Different (comma) difficult

but the angle is difficult, the way the water
falls in mists, and the groups going past or each wearing hats and spinning
in the rain. and the water
is adjusted and a man goes out alone and each structure is a new
informed place and the tree has been trimmed (topped off) and some of its branches
yellowed. so what will be done
there. and the bench on display and the way (the dragonflies are), the cedar
of the tree aching, in fact, the (frolic of the) water
and the past coming on by (with maps, and they don't know where they're going)
so that path is sunny and damp at the same time. so that patch
has dried up and that arc of water
keeps moving in circles (spinning), showing off. it's not hard
to appreciate the scene, the way everything surrounds it. (you can't
plan your life around the paths. you can't.) (and you can't see
how it could have gone differently. these meadows. these fields. these treed
pastures. the clicking motion of above them) (do I want
to enter the building?) can I predict which drop, which mist
will develop? I say the forest. I say
the trees are here, and I with them. I say if it's developed (the development) too far along
there it is. (there is my pasture). (I call out, alone, to be sure)

And

if there's a distinctive
pattern, the olive-glossiness
of the leaves (and the sun's
reflection in them, in
the afternoon), the reasons
why I chose you (beautiful
one), and (emotional) being
charged. the aspect of
(the skin, the leaves)
the changing day, the passing
cars, the where in the afternoon

Because I wanted to be on the path

I saw something there in the brush (and hoped
it would come back, pacing), what hops
in the dry-leaf-ground-cover, simple branches
perpendicular from the ground (wanting something, sunlight
on this dim day) and I want to see what lives
among them, for it to be revealed (do I hear it coming?
if I am still enough). before, exactly, the leaves
drop one or two from above. the blooms (over-
blown) cast out. a bird makes it happen, a squirrel, hum
of the bees (should I leave?) sudden. up high. near
the fruit. and a general rattling, a combined dropping, kneeling
shifting (reclining, breaking) as the sun moves about
if you look at it. it moves—if you look at it it falls. dear
treed terrarium, tiny (domed) world—something moved
inside, moved below, anyone who's listening
would know it's there (searching) about, unquiet like
the blue bird we saw once, rare (in our own piece
of land, our real country) everywhere, on each branch
on every fencepost, cantilevered, and about to return (again)

If anyone is to ask

we cross a road, we cross a street, we've been let
out of doors and are happy enough—can anyone tell
(tell me, tell me not to go alone, to keep my hands
ready) where? it all sounds like something alive, the trees
and the grass and the breeze, and already the leaves
(that we would like to eat) are drooping, folding in
the failed outdoors, the day that begins in a mist settled
under the high sun. the vibrations of the building
(a distant croak? an outside beetle) near the back
of my neck, which feels rough. what we want to know
is to ask, a soothing way to a (single) answer, not bursting
up into the sky or rattling the tops off the railings, forgotten
forgotten in the low bushes by the only bird (whose face
we recognize, who has come home many times, with its small
head). the mistakes can come (we don't want left, we want
to crease them over, fold into the perfect five-pointed-star
of ideal angled beauty) and circle the puddle around the drain
if they'll ask them to you, your name, your work, how often
we may visit the future, if invited, already, to fill those gaps

In the fog, the world

green leaves that fade and shrink, the world
I could imagine, the water
there, near the depression of the path, the sadness
of the speaker, when squirrels
and other birds disrupt the leaves. the water
moves in circular motions, each falling
heavily, a blue-blanketed carriage rolls by—because
who will know when I look
up, when I might be moved to look up again—the shudderings
there, the nearing. find me the way to the water—the hose
the faucet, the line—and shut off
these fidgetings. you take the sentimentality out, you fake
the aching watching, you
prefer jealousy over water's soft flow, the determined
movement of machines and we're
left in the leaf-mulch, with the smallest flying
bugs and the droppings of the unfortunate
animal, while past the hedge the ladies in white hats
collect plant trimmings—into their
pop-up laundry hampers—cooing over butterflies
and the low, cool breeze and, tapped
into the role of politeness, look sneakily
over the ends of the hill to see exactly—precisely—
how the water falls below it

You who wouldn't survive, otherwise

plant the tree that wouldn't survive, and wonder
since you've wandered so far from it, what you can tell
from rooftops and fencelines, manipulated cedars, small-blooming
grasses (mustards) in the slow wind, against the sky. what a wonder
isn't. and it's so dry—(unless you water the tree) the human backed up
right (up) to it. not enough shadow, we think, weeds are growing
in, skittering happily across (a nurse tree, a parasite, growth
upon a growth) and anywhere we decide to sit would be good (enough)

no. did you see someone? did you hear? (mockingbird. slim-
feathered tree). the green cart in secret by the manzanita
that hides the path, the road, leafmeal. striking too soon
in the distance. behind my right shoulder, a branch falling, tree
lifting, the crack of midafternoon with the shadows
(jostling, maneuvering) about. flirting bee. (tumbled butterfly)
white-lipped. the calm-enough forest. the quiet-enough perch
(you couldn't have found it. sometimes, what crawls
there. what scatters). oh the purples, o the yellows, entire nuts
in the scat, the scat, the scat itself. the colors of this week. the dirt
road of day, bent neck, helpful map, the lost (location). sentimental
you? my habit formed sufficiently that (I get swarmed, lightly)

Reliving below and above

always a thing moving: animals, wind, manzanita, stream
(which should not be so, dry stream, snow run-off, traipsing
along), always, the sound of the machines, the birds. lone limb
or clear sky, rocks of many sizes. ready for discovery, following
a trail, the wind blows so, I wonder when (someone will come)
if I am here moving along (or in the silence before a step, before
taking a step). and the path blocked off from traffic, a trail
so those voices carry—to see something (droll), to see the place
askew, switchbacks on the low ground (I've gone there, heard
those bees—that humming uncovering, sound alighting beneath
the trees, on that turn against the cliff). you ask when we'll go
if we live, so in the broad leaves, in the pine-needled (ponderosa)
in low agave… the leaves on the land decompose: their veins
show through, they look torn, they turn to dirt. elements fall apart
and in the afternoon heat, droop, to the ground, hang (with shouts
across them, or the trill of the animal draping over) in the breeze
unrelievable, in slow motion (in the lake mirage. and the dust
that kicks up) (the voices, steps without a vantage point) below

Maybe next week, maybe the week after

the meadow wrapped in plastic, some place I hadn't known, maybe
an insect (animal) peeking out from under. a leaf spinning
on a web, simple in the air, even among those bees, so many
on the blue flowers, behind them, over the light (and hairy) moss. on
a shining rock, ants astride the path, the hose, the seeing that occurs
(because I'm here. because birds' voices travel) in the always accidental
discovery (the bee that has discovered me). gooseberry? mountain
mahogany? voices out and up behind them? most likely not

(I'm) seated, or imagining

the clicking wire, the cricket (who escapes. who gets
      caught) preparing for some ceremony
under the white tent, in the tall grass, determined
      by the gravel-tossed plastic sheeting, actually
(within the short-logged boundary. the pre-planned benches)
      unable to distinguish music from wind, what comes on
from beyond. seated, or imagining (imaginary) that one
      (if not the other) will end, will move along, has
gone now. the gravel path gives enough (soft for
      prints, slogging through, as ocean is related
to pine, that strong determined smell). of course
      there's sun here. it's been made. the chirping developed
and admired. placed, seeking its own disturbance, its method
      my entry (and the twig falls. the loped ear droops)

Testing, or the group of them

hidden beneath the brim, something pokes from the path
slightly dangerous. these shaped twigs which only grow
unsightly, testing the mud, if the group of them forward, forward
forward enough. one leaf turned orange, mountainous air, the waterfall they speak of
bedded down (near) the lawn. deserving the perfect crown, the beautiful
hat, the pool of bent reeds—don't forget, along the sculpted hedges
the heads reflecting left and tilting up (*I haven't been here before*), and they're
coming, the helicopters, retreating (the pack birds) to the next
shady layabout, clear from the voices, near the dry leaves
(*I wouldn't ask you to forget me*, a letter could be distraction
for the scraping that occurs) and the new
green tops, fresh for fall

Of the tree in the path

you can't be alone in the garden, either
with your cane, your easel, with your
hose (flitting to the sound of the freeway
kneeling the birds in the grass, darkly looking
at your hobbies), too heavy for the weather
the local (culture), something to be done
to the trees, dear sunken trunks, as if
you're somewhere else (you've lost the entrance)
shaded beneath planks like a liquid
among the roots. the last gasp of the trail
the path, the number of women here, that you
couldn't help but know. act, drag, the casting
of the wind (too delicate, dear) to rustle much
of such a tree

Up the tree or down the tree

                                 running along the wire, past
the periphery, though the leaves on the ground (a dry crunch, deep
pleasure). night comes, along after the day and the weather
is back again, the hum of distance, and who needs
what I'll send them to, or when, in the open field, where
the animals are small and mild, natural. they flirt
with me after all, admiring my hair and my boundaries
and my tired age
                            in my head, and all around it, the gentle
shaking, there, down from the limbs, on the soil, the ground
in the path where it smells like peaches, green curry, spicy
bay. I haven't made one, I never found one, I sat still
all day and tried not to let anyone see in the heart (of the space)
of the clearing, the slight wind that stalls just nearby, there

There has been a storm

along the path of the-place-I-hadn't-
gone-to (arrived at) before, or the birds
that lead me to the-spot-that-didn't-
exist before, near that patch of (the land
of) dormant flowers, the way to fill
my days, the red shooting-stars and the quaint
leaves. it's clear there has been a storm, the kind
that blows fall back to summer in the palms
splayed along (along) the ground or the sun
out above or the mess beside the treeline (treeline) so pleased
to recover here, looking happily to the slight(ly) breezes
in the rabbit-brush, the naturalistic recreation of an afternoon slipping
the length of, about to spear (appear) me from the down the path—I hear it

(cage) (tree-cage)

the light-headedness
of those darting
beneath the tree (cage)
(tree-cage), the quail
rustling, the jutting
the yellow leaf
to signal the beginning
of the turning, the motion
about to arrive
(I read this
I sat in the shadow.)

Found out, acted upon

seen from above, seen from that slick crossing, deep
in the weedening weeds, sly insect drama. so that half
are against and there is the frame (and I obscure
it like this, and I do) and here is the photo
the picture within, the terrified jumper, holding-to
bedding down (the leaves), the morning rush and the small
and early afternoon (how will I do it better?). each one
pounded atop, each sound hidden within, the easement
(we would say: between the floorboards, among the spun
leaves, in the crush of carapace, the distraction created, small
quiet pile) of waiting to be released again, could not frown
without, and the rain above, the rain that breeds
the secret shadow (swollen, swollen) afraid to appear
down near the river (which is actually a rivulet in the path
and nothing swims there) and the peach tree and the lost yard
of yesterday's (daydream) (cinema). forgetful in the hall
under the clutter of branches (the sun, hailing), the scene
and a hair that rears and grows, an anemic conclusion
on the open plain (that is obscured by trees, and where the sky
is also obscured) along of grass, along of sharp weeds
and thin sticks along the edge of the circle containing its piece

I recognized the first turn

I had been once before, I recognized
the fast road, the quick turns, the delirious
aftereffects of the curves. the view. the diminished
sense of space, the birds that shook apart the trees, the unreason
of low agaves creeping across the hills, the movement
there. was one of space, of mountain leaves, in fall, a gesture
of saddened escape (futile progress, if not for this: the birds). and
no one was there—the path was empty, the bench
rattled slightly with my pen, there was no conforming to it, there was no sky
(beyond the mist, beyond my face bloated big, and the clear windows). everyone
saw. there was no one there

                          how many are mine, of the four-to-five leaves left
hanging still? you should know (and you should act like it, the birds
seem to gesture, I've been here all day
I live in a house. the moment is mine). the eight
left leaves are orange. they are red, they are
turning. we've stopped (we've slowed down, the road
shifts, the asphalt creeps, potted). would I call this my house?
would I want to wait here? pudgy bird, distracted robin. am I
where you wanted to rest? a small thing, but enough
unlikely enough, home. dirt and dust (arising) all the way through. no one
is here but it's not empty. ragged enough perch. enough of the way
the land works: rises and falls. enough of the unfairness
of the roads. your skepticism is available, noted. it's enough. it is old. (the bypass
is headed my way, the rise of the hill there, and the blink of the sky)

***

(ladies vary)

they are so lovely and they cannot get out.

they are lovely, yet they cannot get out.

they are so lovely so they cannot get out.

so they are lovely, but they cannot get out.

they are lovely, for they cannot get out.

they are so lovely, for they cannot get out.

but they are so lovely they cannot get out.

so they are so lovely, so they cannot get out.

they are lovely, or they cannot get out.

they are so lovely, and they cannot get out.

They trail there, they trail

it was the one yellow thing in the gray-green
world, the one with narrow curling tendrils, the one reaching
out, even, the one hummingbird shooting past, knee-height, yellow exactly like
(the tree-poppy, a native species), yellow as the robin's red under-
side (reflecting off the soft dirt, soft peat). but not yellow
as the leaf there, as twisting as the soft air, the boundless animals over
short twigs, picking up the short twigs and carrying them along
in their short arms, short beaks. who drift in patterns, in waves
of sound, and echoes and cannons of them, the sirens
that (in effect) have been surrounded by (the dull roar of yellow) the only lacy
thing, the only fine thing, the only petaled thing. the gray
path slowly curving to the right, to the left, curving away, the only only
soft thing

           when it is quiet then the birds. (when it is still then the yellow)

what's closer (I have turned in all directions. I have lifted
up the leaf, pushed aside the branches, listened to the range, looked
for the small birds and the large birds and the soft animals and the hard
even off the trail, the rocks. even the pined twigs, browned
along the edge, even the distance, the total absence of clouds, the sighing
branches, the pleading birds)? what is closer is I am still here

Dispelling the shadows

the bent leaves and simple sun. a slight blush
underside the boughs, subtle shading of that flesh. the clouds
and the new form of water, ducking past, seeking beneath
as if dried flowers on the tips still reach up (as if
there's sun there) to avoid the crowd, to show off, to start
again

they are diffused (crushed), hanging there. attracting
bees, the consent (of a purposeful language, an aggressive
flower, uncontrolled. but wood is always
warmer, we (always) know, looking for tracks in the leaves
there, compelling movements (in the cool afternoon)
(the high-skied shadowless afternoon)), cooing, asking for
some treatment

yes (yea) for something has come, a low shuffling, the muted
voices, they come in a pack, wolves, they descend
on the valley, in the garden. trailing a certain smell (of the kind
not yet touched). the breezes astound, the lifting
types of air they bring, the circular clearing around each tree
the untrue fact left unnoticed: it's empty. the green bits
shooting up are not leaves in the end, are not
what we had anticipated

if it is the same path, after all, if it is the same tree (the same
needles) should we not be sorry? should we not
disengage?

(a a aviary)

they, they cannot get out
their breasts, they trail among the azaleas
their lashes, they lift

this sugar, the sugar

they inquire, their fingers shift

their visitor, this lump of sugar

there is a tremor, these tassels, their impatience
their recompose, their ruffles

What would you like us to be

lovers? children? tall birds claiming
the uppermost branches. the bounty
littering the ground. where
would you like us to go? how would you
like us to attend? (call to ease, a shadow
pushing through the blossoms. imagining
the path) charming, cheerful, not hanging
much on the details (the bird uses its beak
to disconnect the flower. the petals flung
from the tree) (whole blooms of them, tossing
pink to the ground.) (nothing has gotten
more beautiful) (unless it's a secret
entrance). (exit.)

(lies in an aviary)

it is so sweet   sugar, the sugar

a flock of satin curves

sedately folded,   a diamond

a woman's whole existence

As if on clouds, waiting

voices down the path, in the trees, unconsciousness
even clinging to the branches in the chill
of them (if you hold the tree, palm up
it's cool and appropriate to touch). the single
moment, the moving shade (roving air) as voices
glide through, as a face (beckons) at some distance
sliding in (abruptly) through the fresh sky
(meaty) flowers, dangling bare branches against
the green hills, the sloped downfalls, what I will
find in the morning, holding till, shrugging off, calling
to (we cannot get lost here) (the population
abounds) a single shade in the dirt, falling open
there upon it

tense in the dry leaves, coarse
in the long grass (an orange rind, a litter, of opened
fruits), a scattering as the clouds did not (did not)
come, the sky reflected in the ground, by birds
holding out for (sweet olive) afternoon (around
the lagoon, the false island)

Here is love

in the street, beneath the tree, upon
the sidewalk, in the arms, in the branches
between the clouds, in the shade, in
the morning, against the curtain, below
the sunlight, against the flowers, across the lawn
among the blue-pincushions, the biting lilies, the stranded
screen, against the rock wall, in the awning
beneath the draperies, in the meadow, against the river
in the dust there, in the earth, among the daylight, the ivied
leaves, within the boundaries, up the driveway
after the culvert, under the shelving, in the garden, circled
by scenery, in the sunlight, in the breeze, under the blue-
spruce, against the fan-palm, in the grove
adrift in safety, wrapped by endlines, for an occasion, inside
the park, beyond the entrance in the clearing, in the dry river
below the hawk-bleat, on the road, in the density, in the coming-upon-it
in the woodland, in the garden, in the cleared land, among the policies
of the soil, in the reclaiming, by the water, beyond the watchers, in the care
by the entrance, in the thick-of-it, beneath bare branches, in the leaves, adjoining
the causeway, in the lighting, in the spy glass, in the sanity, in the asking
along the road, in the coming in the distance, in the observed, near the maple, beside
the sunlight, in the strewn leaves, among the animals, in the night sounds, in the leaving
by the open field, in the asking, in the description, in the enclosure, by the deed

(dies an aviary)

they are so lovely
                    their breasts
they trail their lacy

their lashes   they lift

solitaires on their fingers shift up and down

                        waiting

 running to eat
                        very wistfully

A light as forgotten (to us)

as gnats flitting in the tall grasses, bolster of the shallow ponds, low breezes
among the reeds in the forgotten land. starred aspen, starry, the opening
of the meadow: green with wisps looking upwards, reaching
for their place (when I'm gone, you'll need a place to be, who comes
too close, who doesn't know better), the flowers haven't yet forced
their way up. to touch them, unkind torsos themselves upon the opened wood
white trunks, bare—as forgotten as the dried, curled leaf, folded into
a shell, curled in the middle, along the ends, folded over. it throws
into relief, it does: dark hummingbird among the small yellows, black-winged
butterfly in the light garden, helicopter churning above the (leaf meal) (bird
step) (grasses) blue-eyed grasses

Their impatience—to be satisfied

with a word, a seed, a mown piece
a wallow in soft damp dirt. the bulbs
become leaves, the petals the branches, the lip
of the fence lifts gently with the breeze, despite
the undergrowth, its peckishness, an uncertain
future

      these tassels, small greens, and their
impatience. the slow wind in the canyon, startling the fresh
leaves, tangle in the river (the canyon, the rocks, the low flitting
forms), the lost ocean, the low lands, the river, unnameable
houses, unlivable

      the single leaf sheening, holding forth
in the sunlight (a tough departure, a taking-leave-of)
cunning. blushed, (the blossoms gone) sidled against
and tramped in, to temper growth and leakage and
fortune

***

PROCESS NOTE

Early on in my process of conceptualizing these poems, Mina Loy's short prose poem "Ladies in an Aviary" leapt onto my desk to suggest itself as an organizing principle, a happy coincidence, a difficult imagination, a devastating image. Loy's description of women whose "breasts are pouting" (line 1), posing as prize birds inside a cage, watched by onlookers, and waiting for men to select and adorn them, as "love...'tis a woman's whole existence" (line 12), resonated with the themes of enclosure and identification with the natural world already echoing through my work. As gardens and natural enclosures—the location of the poems in my series—are often considered feminine or feminized spaces, I appreciated that Loy's poem, with its "sugar of fictitious values" (line 5) and its "nasty sweep of feathers" (line 16), added both recognition and scathing assessment of such a space.

I found Loy's prose poem compelling, engaging, and strange. In Loy's words I also discovered possibilities for extending my own language. I use two main methods to incorporate language from her "Ladies in an Aviary." The first is akin to collage: erasing, alphabetizing, re-arranging, and otherwise permutating Loy's language to create new poems. My poem "(ladies in an aviary)" is composed by alphabetizing all the words in Loy's "Ladies...," making four columns of the alphabetized language, and creating a new poem by reading across the columns. A later poem, "(vary)," uses a similar permutation, working through Loy's language alphabetically—and selectively—beginning with "aviary" and ending with "sugar." These processes highlight elements of Loy's composition, like the repeated use of the word "sugar," or the distinctiveness of certain letters and sounds. When Loy's "man who / brings sugar to the cage" (lines 3-4) becomes my "man, man, massive" (line 17), the man takes on figurative weight, becomes imposing, and in juxtaposition with the previous line "love, lovely, lump" (16), sexual. In other Loy-languaged poems in this series I continue using methods of repetition and variation, curated omission, and visual erasure procedures.

For the second method used to join "Ladies in an Aviary" and my (*aviary*), I select phrases from Loy's poem as titles for my own pieces; the first sentence of her prose poem, "They are so lovely and they cannot get out," becomes the title of my own poem. Excerpts from subsequent sentences become, for example, my titles "That flat look at the naïve" and "It is so sweet this sugar, the sugar." These titles were selected prior to the drafting process so that Loy's language would directly influence the poems that follow. However, not every word of Loy's "Ladies in an Aviary" is represented through my titles, nor can every word be found, in any sensical way, in the poems that make up my series. Loy's prose poem is not represented in (*aviary*) in its entirety and would be difficult to reconstruct from its fragments.

Loy's "Ladies in an Aviary" is itself an amalgamation of fragments found in the archives at Yale's Beinecke Library. According to Roger L. Conover, editor of the collection where Loy's prose poem appears, "Ladies in an Aviary" "is improvised from unpublished notes, prose fragments, or drafts found in M.L.'s folders" (329). This poem can be found in my copy of *The Last Lunar Baedeker* (Jargon Society, 1982), but it is omitted from later editions. It is not included, for example, in the subsequent publication of Loy's poems, *The Lost Lunar Baedeker: Poems of Mina Loy*, also edited by Roger L. Conover (FSG, 1997).

My work with Loy's words in (*aviary*) builds from this earlier textual manipulation of her "Ladies in an Aviary," a poem published first—and, I believe, solely—as one of six "improvised" compositions in Conover's section subtitled "Ready Mades" (311-322) in *The Last Lunar Baedeker*. Is "Ladies in an Aviary," then, a poem by Mina Loy or a poem by Roger L. Conover? Is my poem "(vary)" a poem by Mina Loy? by Roger L. Conover? by Genevieve Kaplan? My work with Loy's "Ladies in an Aviary" is essentially that of un-collaging and/or re-collaging a poem that was only ever a collage. And what is collage but highlighting and juxtaposition? A re-framing of one object within the context of another?

You can read my *(aviary)*. You can read Conover's "Ready Mades" in his 1982 edition of Loy's poems. You can consider the work of The Jargon Society. You can look at various boxes in the Mina Loy Collection at the Beinecke Library. Perhaps you'll find some papers titled "Ladies in the Aviary" that are not poems but consist of an unpublished chapter, an unpublished novel.[1] You can look at all of it, or none. Perhaps you'll be moved to create new poems, collages, ephemeras, aviaries.

---

[1] Depending who you ask. Erin Hollis describes Ladies in the Aviary as "one of Loy's attempted novels" (221) in her 2003 dissertation *Textual collisions: the writing process and the Modernist experiment*; Jacinta Kelly refers to "Ladies in an Aviary" as a chapter from one of Loy's unpublished novels (13) in her 2012 article "Purging the Birdcage: The Dissolution of Space in Mina Loy's Poetry."

ACKNOWLEDGMENTS

I am grateful to the following journals that published poems included in this manuscript, sometimes in different versions: *Dream Pop Press*, *Galatea Resurrects: A Poetry Engagement*, *G U E S T [a journal of guest editors]*, *H_NGM_N*, *Manor House Quarterly*, *Map Literary*, *Moria*, *Rhino*, *Small P[o]rtions*, *Spiral Orb*, *Sugar House Review*, *TAB: The Journal of Poetry and Poetics*, *Terrain.org: A Journal of the Built + Natural Environments*, *Thrush*, *We are so happy to know something*, *Western Humanities Review*, *Women's Studies: An Interdisciplinary Journal*, *Word/For Word*, and *Yew*.

"A swift (quick) justice," "Shift up and down the wires (that close them in)," and "Apart from its pleas" were published on the Woodland Pattern Book Center website, in advance of a reading. "Here is love" appeared as a site-specific woven installation in Pasadena, California in May 2017. You can read an early process discussion of some of the poems in this manuscript, "Un-Collage, Excise, Re-Collage: 'Ladies in an Aviary,'" in *Opon*; this essay is the basis for my "Process Note." My chapbook *In an aviary* is available from Grey Book Press.

The poems with parenthetical titles in sections two and four are composed solely of language from Mina Loy's prose poem / "Ladies in an Aviary," one of Roger Conover's "Ready Mades," which can be found on p. 316 in his 1982 edition of Mina Loy's collected poems, *The Last Lunar Baedeker* (Highlands, North Carolina: The Jargon Society).

Many of these poems were composed in private and public garden spaces across southern California, including Rancho Santa Ana Botanic Garden; the Huntington Library, Art Collections, and Botanical Gardens; and the Los Angeles County Arboretum and Botanic Garden. I was lucky to have received a fellowship from the University of Southern California during the early stages of drafting this manuscript, which allowed me to think and write in these locations.

Many thanks to my family and friends who have encouraged and supported me during the long journey this book has taken, especially to my partner Sean Bernard, and to the students, faculty, and staff at the University of Southern California. Endless gratitude to Laura Cesarco Eglin, for her vision of—and dedication to—this project, and to everyone at Veliz Books, for making it come alive.